salmonpoetry

Publishing Irish & International
Poetry Since 1981

PRAISE FOR GABRIEL FITZMAURICE'S POEMS FOR CHILDREN

'[E]xtraordinary… A child that reads Fitzmaurice will be a child that loves poetry.'
OLIVIA HOPE, Children's Books Ireland

'The Fitzmaurice children's poems are superb.'
SEAMUS CASHMAN, The Irish Catholic

'[T]he Irish A.A. Milne.'
DECLAN KIBERD, The Sunday Tribune

'Ireland's favourite poet for children.'
CLAIRE RANSON, Best Books!

'[F]ull of real spontaneous fun.'
TED HUGHES

Katie

Poems for the Young and Young at Heart

Gabriel Fitzmaurice

Published in 2019 by
Salmon Poetry
Cliffs of Moher, County Clare, Ireland
Website: www.salmonpoetry.com
Email: info@salmonpoetry.com

ISBN 978-1-912561-79-7

COVER PHOTOGRAPHS: *Brenda and Nessa Fitzmaurice*
COVER DESIGN & TYPESETTING: *Siobhán Hutson*
AUTHOR PHOTO: *Tom Moore*

Printed in Ireland by Sprint Print

Salmon Poetry gratefully acknowledges the support of
The Arts Council / An Chomhairle Ealaoín

To Katie
With love from Grandad

Contents

"Grandad,
you have loads of jobs
but the best job you have
is being my Grandad"

Katie (8)

21 April, 2018

Good Morning, Katie!

Is there anything as happy
As a baby just awake
From a good night's sleep in dreamland?
You watch the baby take
Her bottle from her mammy
And when the milk runs out
Baby takes her piggy-toes
And puts them in her mouth;

Her mammy cuddles Katie
And says a little prayer
That Katie will be safe today –
Then Katie pulls her hair!
For Katie is our baby
All blue eyes and curls
And we wouldn't swap our Katie
For the whole wide world.

No! We wouldn't swap our Katie
For the whole wide world.

Happy

Me and Katie and Buttons,
Mammy gone away,
Me and Katie and Buttons
Play.

Katie claps her handies,
Buttons pumps her paws,
Grandad loves his Katie.
We're happy just because.

Katie is Coming

We're all looking forward to Katie
(And no-one at all more than I),
We're all looking forward to Katie
For Katie's our grandchild, our joy;

She'll come with her mammy to our house,
We'll feed her, change nappies and play
Oh! Katie makes each day a Sunday
And Katie is coming today
She is.
Katie is coming today.

Eating Grandad's Books

Katie nibbles Grandad's books
(She's nearly one year old),
Katie nibbles Grandad's books,
It's not that she's being bold –

She loves the taste of paper
And what can Grandad say
Except he hopes she'll take to books
And read them some fine day.

The Terrible Twos

Nana says I'm good as gold
But I won't do what I'm told
'Cos I'm bold.

I'M BOLD!

When I Get Tired of Shopping

When I get tired of shopping
I say "I have a pooh"
And Nana stops shopping
And takes me to the loo.

Every time that we go shopping,
Every shop that we go through
When I get tired of shopping
I say "I have a pooh";

And every time I say it,
Nana has no choice
But to take me to the toilet
And be very nice

To the shop assistant
Who shows us to the loo
Though it's not a public toilet
And though I have no pooh

When I get tired of shopping
I say "I have a pooh"
And Nana has to take me
Always to the loo
'Cos now I'm out of nappies.
No nappies now.

I'm two.

Let's Pretend

Pretend that I'm a baby
With a nappy on my bum,
Pretend that I'm a baby,
Come on, Grandad! Come on!

Pretend that I'm a baby
Though now I'm nearly three,
Come on, come on, Grandad!
Come on and play with me.

It's great fun being a baby,
Grandad you're my friend,
It's great fun being a baby.
Come on! Let's pretend.

Grandad's Best Girl
is Growing Up

She didn't play with me today
(We always played before)
'Cos Katie's nearly three years old
And Patsy's four;

She didn't play with me today,
She took her leave of me
'Cos Patsy is her best friend now
That Katie's nearly three.
Yes! Patsy is her best friend now.
That's how it's meant to be.

Stop Looking at Me!

Just what do you think you're looking at?
You're rude as rude can be!
What do you think you're doing?
STOP LOOKING AT ME!

I'm fed up with being looked at
Now that I am three –
You'd think I was a baby!
STOP LOOKING AT ME!

What do you think you're looking at?
Is there nothing else to see?
I'm fed up of being looked at!
STOP LOOKING AT ME!

Watching TV

All morning I've been sitting down
While Mammy's shopping in the town;
Watching TV's very good,
Puts you in a happy mood;
Everything I like to see
Is on this morning on TV
But now I think I've seen enough
Of Scooby Doo and all that stuff.
Oh yes! I've watched enough TV.
Grandad, will you play with me?
PLEASE!

A Little Girl Discusses Her Grandad

I won't kiss my grandad,
Let me tell you why –
Although I'm very fond of him,
Grandad is a boy,
He is.
And I don't kiss boys!

A Little Girl Discusses
Her Daddy

Daddy is my boyfriend,
He's nicer than the rest,
When I grow up I'll marry him
'Cos I love him the best.

Nanas

Nanas give you goodies
When mammies say they can't
'Cos nanas always give you
Exactly what you want
And mammies can't give out to them
'Cos they are very old
And that's why they're allowed to be
Very, very bold.

Nana's Plate

Of all the food I ever ate
The nicest comes from Nana's plate
For nothing tastes quite as good
As a forkful of her food,
Rashers, sausies, bacon, ham,
Bread and butter, bread and jam,
Turnips, parsnips, onions, beans
And every single kind of greens,
Boiled eggs, poached eggs, scrambled, fried
And all the fish in from the tide,
Boiled spuds, baked spuds, roast spuds, chips
(The stuff she says stays on her hips)
And all the different kinds of meat
On Nana's plate are good to eat
For nothing tastes quite as good
As when I eat my Nana's food.

No! nothing tastes quite as good
As when I eat my Nana's food.

Nana Knits Me Jumpers

Nana knits me jumpers,
Sews fairies on my dress,
Nana reads me stories
'Cos Nana is the best;

Nana knits me jumpers
And I wear them just to show
That I am Nana's best girl
And I love her so.

When Grandad Made a Fart

I knew that he would do it,
I said, "Grandad, don't you start"
But he did it anyway –
Grandad made a fart.

He thought that it was funny,
He thought that he was smart,
But I said, "You're disgusting"
When Grandad made a fart.

But he only started laughing
So I said with all my heart,
"Grandad, you're not my friend,
I told you not to fart
And I won't play with you no more
If you make another fart.
GRANDAD!"

Katie and the Dolphin

Fungi is a dolphin,
He lives in Dingle Bay,
I went with Nan to see him
In a boat today.

We sailed from Dingle Harbour,
The boat went up and down
In the big, big water
And very soon the town

Was far, far, far behind us
And we were out at sea
Hoping to see Fungi –
Would he come to me?

And I looked out at the water
Hoping for a peek
At the funny dolphin
Who plays hide-and-seek

In the deep, dark water
With children just like me
When suddenly Nana whispered,
"Look! Look Katie! See!"

Fungi was beside us,
He was jumping up, yippee!
Jumping high into the air
And plunging in the sea;

And he played with us a long time
And it wasn't like pretend –
A real dolphin played with me.
Now Fungi is my friend.

Beds are Good for Sleeping In

Beds are good for sleeping in,
They're also good for play –
You sleep in them at night-time,
You play in them by day;

You jump on them and tumble
Just like a trampoline,
You can play your toys, play pillow fights
And also submarines;

Beds are good for sleeping in,
They're also good for play –
Me and my friends play there
And they're coming here today,
They are,
They're coming here today.
Hurrah!

Fridge

A fridge is only just a fridge
With just a boring door
Until you stick some pictures on,
The kind that children draw

With puppies, kittens, smiling flowers,
A happy girl and boy
And birds and bees and mams and dads
And the sun up in the sky.

A Little Girl Plays with the Figures in the Crib at Christmas

I played with the toys in the crib today –
The cow and the ass lying down in the hay,
The shepherds with their lambs and sheep
And baby Jesus fast asleep,
The three wise men and Joseph too
And Holy Mary dressed in blue:
I played with them all in the crib today.
It's Christmastime! Hurrah! Hurrah!

A Three Year Old Girl Looks Forward to a New Baby

I'm getting a new baby –
He's in my mammy's tummy
And when the doctor gets him out
He will be so funny:

He won't have any hair or teeth
But that will be just fine
And I will play and play with him
'Cos he will be just mine.

A Baby Brother for Katie

The first time I saw Paddy,
I was very shy
But before long I got used to him
And gave him a toy

One of my own teddies,
I placed it by his head
But he was very fast asleep
In his little bed.

Yes, he was very fast asleep,
I rubbed him once or twice
'Cos he's my little brother
And he's very nice;

Yes, he's my little brother
And we love him – yes!
But still I'm Da-Da's little girl
'Cos I'm my dad's princess.

Babysitting

Kate asleep upon my arm,
I keep her snug and safe from harm,
When she wakes we both will play,
Meanwhile I give thanks and pray.
Though the times might think this odd,
She brings me very close to God.
My granddaughter.

Katie

My tomboy is a lady
Now she's nearly five
Full of "please-and-thank-you's";
I'm glad that I'm alive

Just to be with Katie
And to see her grow
Into a little woman,
The nicest one I know.

My Katie.

GABRIEL FITZMAURICE was born, in 1952, in the village of Moyvane, Co. Kerry where he still lives. For over thirty years he taught in the local primary school from which he retired as principal in 2007. He is author of more than sixty books, including collections of poetry in English and Irish as well as several collections of verse for children. He has translated extensively from the Irish and has edited a number of anthologies of poetry in English and Irish. He has published volumes of essays and collections of songs and ballads. Poems of his have been set to music and recorded by Brian Kennedy and performed by the RTÉ Cór na nÓg with the RTÉ National Symphony Orchestra. He frequently broadcasts on radio and television on culture and the arts.

salmonpoetry

Cliffs of Moher, County Clare, Ireland

"Like the sea-run Steelhead salmon that
thrashes upstream to its spawning ground,
then instead of dying, returns to the sea—
Salmon Poetry Press brings precious cargo to
both Ireland and America in the poetry it
publishes, then carries that select work to its
readership against incalculable odds."

TESS GALLAGHER

The Salmon Bookshop
& Literary Centre

Ennistymon, County Clare, Ireland

"Another wonderful Clare outlet."
The Irish Times, 35 Best Independent Bookshops